Alice the Healer

John Ling

AuthorHouse™
1663 Liberty Drive
Bloomington, IN 47403
www.authorhouse.com
Phone: 1-800-839-8640

© *2010 John Ling. All rights reserved.*

No part of this book may be reproduced, stored in a retrieval system, or transmitted by any means without the written permission of the author.

First published by AuthorHouse   10/25/2010

ISBN: 978-1-4520-8132-8 (sc)

Printed in the United States of America

This book is printed on acid-free paper.

Because of the dynamic nature of the Internet, any Web addresses or links contained in this book may have changed since publication and may no longer be valid. The views expressed in this work are solely those of the author and do not necessarily reflect the views of the publisher, and the publisher hereby disclaims any responsibility for them.

Write me a poem.
Make me a song.
Tell me a story
I don't yet know.
Speak to me slowly
of children and schooling.
Tell me how nice it is walking alone.

Not reassurance
but reason I need,
for summer outside
slowing the day.
Me in the same spot
doing the same jobs,
hoping somebody will
feel of my needs.

So write me a poem.
Use some new words.
Paint me some pictures.
Give me some dreams.

By RJ (Alice)

Alice the healer

Alice (R.J.) was a feisty strong and single minded woman, who endured a great deal of suffering. She loved people, and was a generous heart, who gave an enormous amount of pleasure to many. She loved to talk, and she was a great story teller. ("Lubrication")

Alice and I were friends for the last fifteen years of her long life. We met at a writer's group in Huddersfield. She was still able to drive then, but needed a stick to get from the car to the meeting room. She had already by then been coping with rheumatoid arthritis for many years. We arranged to move the group from an upstairs to a downstairs venue.

She loved writing, to which she came late in life. But most of all she loved being among people who liked writing. She thoroughly enjoyed sharing her work with others, and the chance to show off. She enlivened that group. And this despite also being severely deaf, for she also suffered from Meniere's Disease. But you would hardly have known that she had any disability once she sat round that table.

Alice was also a painter, not a very original one, for she mostly painted from photographs. But she loved learning from skilled teachers, and again it was the group that was most important to her. She was a people person above all. Her house was festooned with her paintings, mostly landscapes and birds. ("Alice paints")

A large period of her youth was spent in ballroom dancing. She was athletic and energetic, and went with a group of friends from event to event, making all her own dresses. She was again a popular centre of attention and had many admirers. She also went walking and cycling.

As a child she won a scholarship to the local college. But her father said she could not go because they could not afford the books and other expenses. So instead she was enrolled as an apprentice in one of the local textile mills. She was a quick learner, and very soon rose to a responsible position, learning all sorts of processes in the factory, and in other mills after that. She eventually became one of the first female managers in that industry, and was much sought after, although this did not please some of the men in a traditional male bastion.

Later in her fifties she retrained as a nurse, and became the leader of a special unit within social services, whose job was to provide care in the home for elderly terminally ill patients. She began this by visiting patients on a motorbike, but soon graduated to a mini. She was alone and self supporting at this time. The skills she learnt there she later applied to her own self care.

As her illness gradually took hold, she set herself up in a bungalow near to where she was born. This was modified to suit the needs of a wheelchair user, including the garden, which was rebuilt with a ramp, and with pots and some raised beds to enable her to work in them. She was alone again after her second husband died. ("Out")

She endured the replacement of both knees, but although she tried briefly to begin walking again, she slowly became dependent on the wheelchair, and on her two children and grandchildren, and some visiting carers from social services. ("New knees") In the last ten years she lost most of her hearing and her vision was also affected by the Menieres. Towards the end she could only watch TV with subtitles and no sound. But she left a house full of books, another of her great loves. She was saddened when her eyes and her hands no longer allowed her to read, and the world of music was completely denied her.

Another of her many skills was cooking. She learnt how to cook for several meals at a time, and was thrifty as well as generous. Whenever I visited there was always some freshly made cake or some scones, and she would often share a meal with me. A few weeks before she died she had prepared a full scale Christmas dinner for me and a friend, which cost her a whole day's effort, and a great deal of pain. ("Alice's feast")

She became impatient with many of the people who did for her from social and other services, and dismissed some of them, preferring to do for herself, however long it took. She felt that hardly any of them including the audiological services, who should know better, knew how to, or were prepared to make the effort to speak to a deaf person who needed to lipread. Medics would stand over her while talking, so she could not lipread them, as that meant raising her head to see, which she found too painful. Hospital staff would shout at her, but not in a way she could understand. They would talk to other people about her, but not explain to her personally, so she often came away from a hospital visit not knowing what had happened. ("Alice loses patience")

And during her many stays in hospital she became appalled at the way less able patients were ignored, misunderstood or not fed. Her hospital stays when she was less disabled, were spent in visiting other patients in her wheelchair to cheer them up. ("Taking charge")

In her last years her world was reduced to the house and garden. She loved the garden and all its visitors. She knew by sight all the different birds that visited her bird table, the squirrels that dug up her bulbs, and the seasonal features of all her plants. ("Late afternoon sun") She became content with her lot, despite constant pain, and the increasingly unsuccessful attempts by medics to deal with it.

She had been a staunch member of the local church in her youth, and taught in the Sunday school. There was almost no contact with the church in her old age, but she prayed to her god every day, she said, to give her strength to get through each day. She believed he did so. ("Torch bearer") And she needed it. Most of her neighbours and friends were either dead or fallen away. Disability is unattractive and difficult to deal with, and especially deafness. People are embarrassed by their inability to communicate. ("Fools not suffered")

But she remained gracious and stoical. She even learned how to use a computer in her late seventies, and ordered all her food and goods on the Internet. She also made contact with many silver surfers, and kept up a daily correspondence with several of them. This was my usual way of telling her whether I was able to visit, or for her to request favours, as she could not use the phone. ("Virtual reality")

Alice taught me a lot about life. She found out for herself on the Internet the information she needed to know about her various drugs, and about the progress of her own illness. Eventually she grew tired of being experimented on by the medics, and decided to control her own medication. ("Alice takes control") Know your enemy, she said. Learn its ways, and how to live alongside it. Reduce what you do, but do it in spite of the pain, and however long it takes. Don't stop trying. Never give in. She remained lucid, humorous and always well dressed to the end. Her house was spotless and well ordered.

Alice died in 2010 aged 82. These poems were written over the last ten years of her life, and form a biography of sorts, and a memorial to her. I hope they may give hope and strength to others in her position.

Thanks, Alice. John Ling August 2010

Cover painting by RJ ("Alice paints")

John is a Quaker and a community mediator with Mediation Yorkshire, and also works with the Alternatives to Violence Project. He worked previously as a children's librarian, a teacher of deaf children and a teacher of autistic children. He is the author of two other books –

"I can't do that!" Social stories to help with communication, self care and personal skills. Lucky Duck 2nd ed 2010

"Social stories for kids in conflict" Speechmark 2010

Profits from the sale of this book will go to the charities – National Rheumatoid Arthritis Society (UK) and Menieres Society (UK)

PAIN!

You must excuse me
or not, as you see fit
I don't care I am not
fit to care I do not
care to fit into this chair
into this care I do not fit
this hair hurts my hair
is in pain I complain
hair should not hurt
you cannot comb pain
brush it away like hair
on the shoulder its there
getting bolder making me
feel older stiff and colder
a boulder on my shoulder
pain in the neck in the
head in the brain it's a
brain pain excuse me

Alice waits

for the day to begin
for pills to work
for pain to ease
for legs to move
for kettle to boil
for tea to cool
for head to clear.
For cleaning ladies
dinner ladies
delivery men
dog walker
ambulance driver
for her turn in Physio
for her return home
for a paper boy who forgets
for a gardener who doesn't come
for a Council who take too long
for a builder to call back
for a ramp that's never built.
For a son who is too busy
for a daughter who is too far
for a friend with time
for a phone call
for a night out
for the day to end
for sleep.

New woman

Alice has reinvented herself.
Once out, now in, once fast, now slow,
The god of small things has redesigned every function,
awarded them new places in the hierarchy of chores.
Minor is now major, big a distant memory,
high and far out of bounds,
low and near the new horizons,
now and later the new future.

Alice goes swimming, dancing, cycling,
roaring round the house at one mile an hour,
reversing into door posts, spilling cups of tea,
executing three point turns, wheelies down the hall,
spiders crushed, dogs tail plucked,
paint scratched, glasses broken.

She is Wheelchair Woman, pill popping vandal,
and if she could control her hands,
remember the words, she would scrawl
screaming graffiti on the walls of her body's prison.

HOSTAGE

Alice does her aerobics, one muscle at a time,
those she can move, and those she can't,
in a cacophony of agonies,
from opening bone dry eyes
to getting an arm in a sleeve.

Concentrate, calculate.
Small feats of giant proportions,
negotiations under duress
with the terrorists of pain
who have hijacked the body.
Sometimes there seem to be
more gunmen than passengers,
she is all pain and no body.

But until the pills kick in she keeps a clear head,
thinks through each move, gets alongside the
villain,
learns his ways, speaks his language,
till they rub along together,
journey to the bathroom side by side,
and defying the enemy,
not using the wheelchair footrests
so as to exercise her legs,
her secret plan to keep them in readiness
to use again some day when the siege is over.

Alice's world

Alice drives slowly about her domain
from kitchen to lounge, bedroom to bathroom,
elegant gliding, clean reversing,
one handed steering, no collisions,
teacup, sandwich, poised on her tray.
Knows each small distance, turning space, leg room,
objects sparingly placed, precisely,
none without purpose, all for one person.

People will call, with their expectations,
offering plans for bright little outings,
wheelchair friendly shopping excursions,
gardens, restaurants, walking people's
plans, with walking people's meanings.

But Alice finds meaning within her new means,
for finding is meaning, and meaning is all.
Within these walls her means of survival,
her orderly haven, her take on the world.
Remembers each bird that visits the garden,
its times, its habits, its place in the order.
Watches each plant, its growth and its season,
its colour, scent, texture and shape.
At one with the mixture of pills by the bedside,
the friendly array of paints in her palette,
the warm rough feeling of paper on easel,
and the tentative soft caress of her brush.

Alice paints

In quiet moments,
not the absence of sound,
for torrents in her head
still flow unabated,
but moments of equilibrium
between raw pain and drug oblivion.
Alice takes a drive to a far country,
to the corner where she keeps
sketch pad, pencils, pots and brushes,
takes the pad, finds the page
where she last roamed
out from the airless room
she can never leave unaided,
across an open field of wheat,
ripe for harvest, sky bright,
poppy flared, hotly layered
finely graded corn stalks
receding into distance,
a place of calm, of solitude,
rich in memory, warmth and healing.

She takes her book and brushes
to the window, mixes colours,
crocked knuckles gripping
like an infant, and paints.
As deep lines of pain between
her eyes momently disappear,
knees and shoulders almost relax,
with her brushes Alice shouts,
across a glorious silent landscape.

Alice, a life

Alice has visitors,
functionaries functioning,
offspring who spring off,
keeping a body alive, but none
with nothing but nothing to do,
nothing but life to give.

I wish I was you, she said,
out there, doing things,
as I used to do.
How hard it was to make
my ordinary life sound dull,
when any other life to her
would be so rich.

They do not come.
They cannot bear
to live their lives,
to sit and listen,
ask how are you,
and hear the honest answer.

OUT

When the ramp is built,
when the door is changed
it will open outwards
and outwards she will go,
out to the outside
from the prison of IN
to the dream of OUT.
From pale and stale
to clean and green,
now a concrete concourse
where she used to discourse
with shrub and flower
and trowel and fork.
It will bloom again.
She has ordered seeds,
has planned and plotted.
There will be no weeds.
She will touch and smell,
listen and gaze
and greet passers by
who never came near,
and enjoy their surprise
when they find her still there.
She will reach from her wheelchair
with long handled shears
and potter and poke
and prune and trim,
and slowly forget
how it hurts to bend.
For slowly but slowly
Alice will mend.

Alice thinks

Alice has been thinking all week long
of coffee tables, chairs and power points,
of turning space, text phone and kettle,
a change of use for one square metre,
a calculated ergonomic move,
to make the most of each waking hour,
to fine tune the use of every room
to wheelchair specific, clutter free,
one woman's needs, and one alone,
the house an extension of the body,
the body an extension of the brain,
and rearranging furniture, a need
that takes a week of thinking to achieve.

Alice loses patience

Alice loses patience with the young man
so well paid to sit and flit through
her impressive fat file, asking more fatuous
questions, adding to those already unread
and unanswered.
Questions unasked,
to which she has the answers are these;
How does it feel to be eighty,
to feel weighty through lack of exercise,
to be exercised by ninety minutes in an
ambulance, to wait ninety more in pain
for this ten minute inquisition,
to live with torture every day,
to fight pain to get up, wash, dress,
cook, eat, move about the house, even
to think, to fight not to be reduced
to less than yourself?
His is the pain of not knowing.
Hers is the pain of his impotence.

Pill power

The choice is this –
brain or pain,
will power or pill power.
These paints, these brushes
in eloquent attendance
on the window ledge
she will employ
she will enjoy
while she still can
while the brain is clear
till the pain shrieks
pull down the blinds.
She lays down the brush
takes up the pills
and her window of lucidity
darkens and closes.

Alice's daughter

Alice's daughter's going away
taking a holiday long overdue,
says she will send her a *Norfolk* card,
wonders how her mother will cope.

Alice says "Cards I do not want.
I know well how *Norfolk* looks.
How I cope is my concern.
Your concern is yours, not mine.

I have been where you are now.
But you cannot, will never be, me.
So let our lives stay separate.
I love you. Now go your way."

Something and nothing

This time she lies down on the sofa
not getting up to greet me now.
Steroidal cheeks sag on the cushion.
Empty wheelchair stands in wait.
Subtitled show on silent TV.

I put myself in her line of vision,
someone real, I can talk back.
She lists the bits of her still working,
degrees of pain, eyes that grow dim,
muscles that burn, including *this* one,
thumping the chest with swollen fist
that can hardly grip the spoon for tea.

All gone now, one by one,
dancing, walking, writing, painting.
Just phone, TV, memory and pain.
Those, she says, who still have something
will not see its value till
they know how nothing feels.

Never ask

"Never ask them how they feel.
never let your feelings show."

She struggles cutting food on the plate,
Gripping the fork, spilling the drink

"When changing a dressing of cancerous blood,
or a newly soiled incontinence pad."

from a two litre carton, her son didn't think,
the book that they bought her, too heavy to lift

"You just got on with it and finished the job,
and both of you knew the score," she said.

So we talk about anything, nothing at all.
I tread a fine line as I listen and nod,
I smile, never asking how she feels,
and never once letting my feelings show.

New knees

The letter has come, the date is set.
Checks begun, x-rays, blood pressure,
Heart rate, weight, drug regime.

A litany of pain is set before her –
spinal injection to deaden the legs,
great loss of blood, to be collected

and veined back in, sawing through
femur and tibia, femur and tibia,
three hours of carpentry, metalwork.

They lay out pain on the table, straight,
hard, red and raw. Alice looks it
right in the eye, recognises it,

sees no worse a dragon than
the one on her shoulder, sees
the end of the siege, start of the dream.

She will go with it, grow with it,
already renewed the driving licence,
planned the new car, the holiday.

Prisoner of war

Like a prisoner of war
they try to break her,
make her get up early
crawl through blinding pain
wait the arrival of
uncertain ambulance,
watch for two hours
others go in before her,
say her file is lost,
make a fuss of finding,
squeeze her in then,
ratchet up the tension,
bring new faces, brown,
unpronounceable names,
forget she can't hear,
speak too quickly,
questions not answered,
try to put her off.

Too much gory detail,
epidural injections
tubes for draining blood,
tubes replacing blood,
on your back four days,
solitary confinement,
unspeakable pain,
may not walk again.

They almost succeed.
But they do not know
what real pain is.
They do not reckon
with Alice's spirit.
They do not know
what strength they give,
the power of Alice's anger.

Taking charge

Alice tries hard, with bruised stiff hands
to spoon her soup without spilling a drop,
observes on the opposite side of the ward
delivery of meals on plastic trays
to the unspeaking unhearing unseeing faces
of women whose minds were mislaid in the theatre,
whose families also have quite disappeared.

There being no body whose job is to feed them,
the food stays inside its hygienic containers
till kitchen staff come back to take it away.
This simple device is a lesson to Alice,
whose legs may not work, but whose mind is not dim.
Today she will transfer from bed to the wheelchair,
from wheelchair to toilet and out in the world.

The doctors call out "Where is Alice, she's missing."
The corridors squeak to the tread of her wheels,
as she zooms through the wards making friends of the friendless,
her anger powered battery driving her on.

Not Knowing

How can it be, this long waiting?
This limb limbo, this assumed
patience of the patient, the arrival
sometime between of the ambulance,
collection of the immobiles by the mobile,
the sitting around in wheelchairs,,
filling in of long forms, gathering
information already given, stored somewhere,
not shared, not known, like a new case?

She is more familiar with them
than they with her. Upstairs, elsewhere,
others have invaded her body,
penetrated veins, filled her with drugs,
experimented, recorded, increased,
reduced, and cut her, removed bones,
replaced with nylon and metal,
sent her home, handed her on.

Now she is a blank sheet again.
They do not see before them, the fear
she overcame, the pain she endured,
the hope she invested, the indignity,
the anger she swallows, anger
for the ignorance, for the waiting,
waiting to be taught, what she used
to know, how to walk again.

Small earthquake in Huddersfield

Traffic continued to flow,
no cracks in the tarmac.
Windows were not shattered,
water pipes un-ruptured,
electricity not cut off.
Not a ripple on the bird bath,
except for two smart magpies
who preened in the usual way.
Pictures stayed on their hooks,
teacups stayed on the table,
emitting the faintest rattle.
Chair legs creaked with tension.
Cushions held their breath.
Curtains faintly fluttered,
as Alice stood -
gripped her new metal frame,
took two steps and two more,
eight out, eight back,
a giant wobbling toddler,
grinning her "look at me" face,
walking her "look at me " walk,
walking,
WALKING,
walking her "look at me" walk.

Fools not suffered

In exchange for the return of the legs,
now the ears take on the mantle of
principal organ for confoundment of
strangers, the chastening of relatives,
and embarrassment of officials.
Only a select few speak in the right
frequency. Others made to say merely
yes or no, their natural argot being
a foreign language. Some are allowed to
listen, as Alice speaks her needs. And one
chosen friend, whom ironically she has
never seen, manages long chats on the
phone, like a love struck youth, no problem.

Doctors glimpsing her past, from fat files
in their slim hands, are lost in her present.
She is utterly Other, even to the white coats
in the department of Oto-Rhino-Laryngology,
eloquent in knowledge of the causes of deafness,
totally ignorant in communicating with the deaf.

Callers who merely call are left standing outside,
surprised by flashing lights and buzzers, tales
of the unexpected untold, unreadable lips unread,
the officious deflated, incompetents dismissed,
fools not suffered.

Alice takes control

One day Alice wakes up
as if from a long sleep
in a dark and distant place
where she had drifted
between dumbing pain
and dumber oblivion.
And seeing before her
consultants consulting
about a new drug
not yet tested
nor approved,
would she like ...
to be your guinea pig?
No I would not.
From now on I am
neither trial nor error.
Not a piece of wood
for you to stick pins in.
This is Alice's body.
Alice lives in here.
Alice knows the pain
this body can endure.
Alice has a brain
which she will employ
in her own consultancy.
Her rubber wheels swish
down the long corridor
to await the ambulance
for the very last time.

Late delivery

Those who deliver late,
medicines, groceries,
incontinence pads,
for whom an hour or so over
is neither here nor there,
have no concept of the stress
caused by moving just a little,
the parameters of expected time,
the pillars that keep the day
from collapsing around her.

To know that when buzzers and bulbs
erupt at 3.30 it will not be
an unpredicted guest. To plan
not to be asleep, or in the toilet,
to be dressed, respectable, not with
hands in the sink or the mixing bowl.
To be ready. To appear normal.
To be calm and polite.
To be Alice.

To be Alice
is to be calm, polite, ready,
organised, smiling, cheerful.
To have slept just long enough
so as to appear alert enough
to chat with visitors welcome or not.
To have had pills at the right time
to create an island of less pain,
sufficient to put the kettle on,
get out the cake and make tea,
to struggle with half heard half
understood conversation,
without loss of dignity.
Even to deal courteously
through gritted teeth
with those who deliver late.

Infusion

I don't often talk about it, says Alice,
holding my gaze unflinchingly.
A hollow needle, a big one, in here,
she points, to where the obtuse tube
abused her blue vein. Several times
they have to try, being young and
needing practice, her veins being old
and needing to resist.
But I say nothing, she says.

Hard to eat, drink or move with
a big needle stuck in your hand
hanging from a tube. Six hours
she sits, in this chair, on these
chromium wheels she uses for legs,
and that after an uncomfortable hour
in an ambulance, while the clear
benign looking foreign liquid
from a bag *this big*, diffuses into
her confused blood all day, as
the young benign foreign staff
rush about, take her blood pressure
every half hour, but say nothing.

The ingress of the silent drug
is preceded by a bag of steroid
that distracts from the shock of
the new, with a shot of the familiar,
so she goes home pain free, relaxed,
crying with relief, moving freely,
planning to walk, drive and holiday again.

Then after a few days, she finds the
Superdrug has gone the way of
all the others, feeling like lead

in her veins, travelling down as
she rises, rising up as she goes down.
I don't talk much about it, she says.
Who wants to hear that sort of thing?
Alice smiles bleakly, as the dulled pain
lurks in unused corners of her body,
waiting to return in force one day soon.

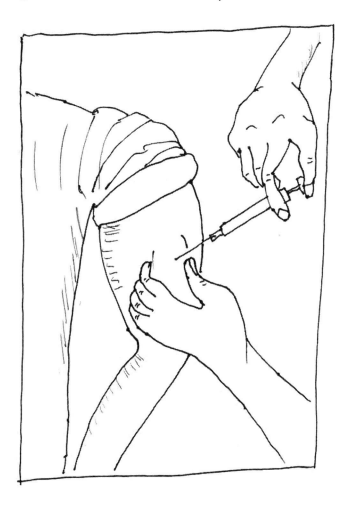

Late afternoon sun

Her steroidal swollen face
can barely raise a smile.
Her voice and hair flat from
weeks of bed and sickness.
Of years of trial and error by
well meaning medics who
treat pain but do not know it,
she has run the gamut,
reached the end point, the It,
thinks will not survive this
time.

Then in mid sentence she laughs,
her eye caught by the extravagant
ablutions of a starling in the bird bath
spraying in the late afternoon sun.
They wait, she says, till I go outside.
Then they come to talk to me,
cock their heads and listen.

A huge ugly crow next, perches briefly
to sip, then to the fence and away.
Beautiful, says Alice, he lives over there
with his wife. They come every day.
We talk of birds and plants, the clematis
full of buds, her arthritic garden more
colourful than a Spalding catalogue.

They should come here, those medics.
Commune with birds and squirrels,
watch water sparkle in the sun,
see how talk gives life to a body,
how a hug compares with a drug.

Skill

Alice enjoys the attention of the woman
who calls to manipulate her body, hoping
for many weeks of tea and banter.
The physio is only deploying one of her
many skills, one which makes a patient
feel like a friend, so that any pain inflicted
will be an unfortunate side effect of her
relationship.
Show me, she implores,
how you walk, giving Alice the urge
to show off, confident that she will be
marked as a hopeless case, and can
sink back into her wheelchair. Instead
she hears, Why aren't you walking?
Why make tea in a wheelchair
when you can do it on foot?

Alice is left alone, debating. Body said
Ooh that hurts, I can't do that.
Brain said, You are disabled, don't do it.
Take the easy way. Use the chair.
Much less tiring. Alice always agreed.
But the physio's words niggled.
Unable to ignore a challenge,
Alice now sits in an arm chair,
walking frame nearby. Wheelchair
now demoted, in another room.
She walks from kitchen to room
to garden, makes tea standing up.
Plans to restore power to dormant legs,
use the wheelchair to go shopping,
walk round the shop. Be able again.

Virtual reality

As her physical body grows through
lack of activity, and her social space
shrinks to these four walls,
Alice's brain sharpens, pushes boundaries
she never crossed or imagined when young.
A silver surfer, on line half the day,
chatting, probing, challenging, seeking
a mental match, a macho thinker, hoping
but not admitting, there will be a soul mate,
a sole male mate, to make her feel whole,
as she once was, whole woman, wholly female.

But the virtual world is a jungle, jumble of
near perfect images, put about by predators,
lonely, once whole men, searching for lost women
to fill vacancies, job spec involving domestic chores,
certain bedtime duties, and of modest intellect.

Herself falling under the spell of more than one,
Alice imagines herself wooed, flattered by
silver tongued punters, who each time she lets slip
her phone number, rush to ascertain her address.
On meeting her, finding themselves tongue tied
helpless, or arrogant and insensitive, unused to
dealing with a female wit sharper than their own,
they depart to lick their wounds and bruised egos.

Alice decides to stay within her safety zone,
play them at their own game, dangle bait,
attract and repel, cast a good fly,
but wait, and stay in control of the line,
then, at the last minute, let them go.

Rules for visitors

R.A. and I live close together
cheek by jowly jowl.
See my deep etched wrinkles,
scars of battle, lines of pain.
See the weight on my body
where muscle once stretched
taut and smooth as a dancers.
No more dancing here, my dear.
These signs speak for themselves,
for I will not speak for them.
There are those who ignore them,
though they have known me
for the whole of their lives,
and should know better.
Those who can read such things,
stay away from my door before
ten in the morning, and after
four in the afternoon. My day
is six hours long for civil chat,
for tolerance of visitors, to whom
I wish to appear not unfriendly,
calm, coherent, tolerant, mobile.
Either side of this window of
opportunity, do not expect
normal rules of engagement.
There, the light is dim, speed
of movement is slow and ragged.
Desperate prayers are prayed.
Mind and matter engage in
murky war games, there is
swearing and groaning, God
knows these things, allows it.
Only He understands.

End game

When she wakes the body says,
Give up now, you're going to die.
Why bother trying any more.
Don't get dressed, think of the pain,
the effort of washing the body,
only held together by pills.
No more now, just let go.
How easy it would be.

But the brain says, No,
I will not give in, will
survive another day,
break the hold of pain,
the mould it wants to squeeze
me into. There are things
still to do, still to say.
Eighty somethings on the Net,
still working out, despite
the prison of the body,
raging against the night.

I know things now, it seems
imperative to pass on to
the children, grandchildren,
though they might not want
to hear it, yet they seem
to know the end is near.
The battle must soon conclude.
Having been an hour dressing,
She lies back on the sofa
to await the big event,
the arrival of the cheery,
life affirming dinner lady.

Dignity

Here again, laid low, so low
she cannot rise from the pillow,
face half concealed in an oxygen mask,
her ancient voice congealed in plastic.
A cough from deep inside rattles like
coals in a sack. Purple fingers peep out
from a bandage enfolding tube ends
that access veins, saving them the
trouble of finding another.

Six jabs in a day she says, pain on pain,
but they have to do it, can't help it,
don't feel it, don't know it, yet so nice,
lovely people. In her agony must still find
reasons to praise, tiny attempt at a smile
flitting across dry lips.
She thanks me
for coming, fondly lists calls and visits
from family, says this may be her last battle,
hopes it is, she is ready, so tired. But amid
the unseemly gadgets, remains dignified,
calm, tolerant. Her free hand gropes
for my arm, swollen fingers rest there
in a feeble, but deep, embrace.

Pain can wait

Where does the anger go? Who gets it?
Waiting so long for an appointment
promised in three weeks, then extended
by three more, due to staff holidays,
as if pain has no sense of time.
Pain can stretch to infinity.
Only she saw it as three weeks long.
An end to pain in three weeks.
A flick of a mouse, and three weeks
of patients' pain stretches to six.
Rescheduled, no apology.
No hard feelings. No soft ones either.
Feelings are not accountable.

Who gets it when the girl at the desk
forgets to order the taxi home?
When an hour stretches to five,
sitting all day in a wheelchair,
no food, no toilet, no company
but old friends pain and boredom.
Long slow drag through the rush hour
strapped in a stiff sprung ambulance,
immobilising the immobile, every
pothole, brake and acceleration
felt in every part of her body.
She's old, disabled and deaf.
Must be used to it by now.
What can we do? Not our job.

Client Alice

Alice in the role of Client is worth exactly
seven breakfasts a week at fifteen minutes,
five lunches at thirty, one cleaning at sixty.
Chat not included, difficult to quantify.
Other bit parts are played by Tesco
van man, five minutes a week, window
cleaner, twenty minutes a month,
ambulance man, a non speaking extra,
and occasional guest appearances by
son, daughter and grandchild or two,
who are in other plays in distant theatres,
but make the occasional dashing entrance
to fetch and carry, do odd jobs, sometimes
of their own choosing, and bang the drum
now and then, in the face of recalcitrant
doctors, chemists and service personnel,
before flying off to resume their careers.

Neighbours do not appear on the cast list,
having long ago forgotten their roles,
apart from waving from a distance.
Very few of the above have lengthy
speaking parts, just the odd routine remark,
and not knowing from Alice's cheery greeting,
that she puts it on through gritted teeth,
disguising her tiredness and pain for their
benefit, so they think she is OK, soothing
their minds ,as they go on their busy way.
Sighing, she switches on her computer,
waits patiently for its slow booting up,
eager to reconnect with the less real,
but more humane, invisible community
of silver surfers, who doggedly continue
to live, all of whom like to be noticed,
and just want someone to talk to.

Torch bearer

She lost them one by one, slowly, in
a long war of attrition, each
power diminished, then removed, testing,
as a torturer does, to see how
much can be stripped away, before

the victim capitulates. The
ballroom dancers legs, that swam, strode
fell and hill, now felled and still, thick
with water, barely able to walk
from kitchen to wheelchair.

Sharp ears of a socialite,
singer, all dead, shut down,
needing lips to read with failing
eyes, the once keen eyes of a
skilled bit passer, now grey

with cataracts, awaiting the
surgeon's knife. Agile fingers of a
seamstress, writer, painter, cook,
now blunt, swollen, bent and stiff.
The lifeblood of a raconteur,

an audience, friends, neighbours, all
gone, unaware, embarrassed
by disability, out of sight,
out of mind. So quiet now
in the shrinking space she inhabits,

no sounds intrude, so
quiet she can hear the pain, it
screams in her head, stings in her
arms, sometimes carves new lines
in her brow.

But, says Alice, my body
is weak, but here –holding a fist to her
chest, in here, I am strong.
I will not give in. Every day
I pray to my god for strength to do

what I have to do, to survive.
Alice prays every day to the
god inside who tortures her body,
tests her resolve, takes away
all her faculties, and remains

the object of her love. The same
hand that turns off all the lights
one by one, leaves a torch for
her to grope about in the semi
darkness.

Lubrication

Like an obsolete mill, the lights going out floor by floor,
the machinery of the body slowly closes down.
Alice knows this, struggles each day to open the gates,
and start up what remains. The oil she needs,
conversation, and audience, is in short supply,
and when supplies arrive, in the form of a visitor,
she goes to work.
The machinery mostly moves
in one direction only; she talks, you listen.
She lubricates herself with talk. The stories
begin slowly, dragged up through bales of pain.
But as the wheels start to turn, the rhythm returns,
the lights flicker again, and for as long as it takes,
she rides the motion. She winds herself up.
Limbs begin to move, laughter provokes gesture.
Someone's knee is patted, wrists squeezed,
her whole body gesticulates. Wheelchair people
don't often get cuddled, but as her party trick
she might stand up and give you one when you leave.
Never mind that you know the stories by heart,
or that nothing happens in the present for weeks.
The past is her story book, her rich canvas, a time
when she belonged, and in the retelling,
she reasserts her humanity.

You the visitor are the medicine, the ears,
the smile that enables her to live again.
Not available on prescription.
Not on Social Services check list.
Not quantifiable. Beyond price.

Risen again,

pneumonia knocked on the head,
sent home to get well enough
to endure the next chemical assault,
another fearful poison that only
fit sufferers can tolerate.
No immunity from pain, infection,
or illness caused by medicines,
she waits in agony, recovering
from the cure, to know whether her
blood will soon be fit to receive
the next infusion. This when it comes,
a two day, six pint affair
for which she is given new pills of
unknown provenance to allay
the shock, that lie on the stomach like
hot coals, and cause the legs to go
to sleep.

Taking control again,
she dumps the pills, legs revive, and feels
three months of pain recede, anticipates
old life returning, talks herself
up, thinks of paint, remembers pictures
stored in her head, plans a new
life canvas, in which ads
will be put in the paper, wannabe
painters will repopulate her lounge,
she will cascade her skills, in
a pain free way. A new artistic
colony, inspired by Alice
van Gogh, whose imagination
knows no bounds, whose veins
run with love,
and other dangerous intoxicants.

Somewhere people

A new old face reappears, in the flesh, in this room,
still in this life, one of the few I had not met from
Alice's childhood narrative, causing her to make more
tea than usual, take more pills than she ought, to gain
more strength for talk, more than a week's ration of
talk,energy and memory, lavished on an old friend.

When I come next day she is ragged at the edges,
losing memory, her storyboard rearranged,
but keen to show me this new character, digs out
photo albums, pages too thin for swollen fingers.
I leaf through, hoping to find yesterday's guest
as a child, a picture filed in Alice's brain,
remembers time and place, she sees it clearly,
but the present eludes her. She is not found.

Each page reveals more memories, flickering before
her
like old silent films. She winds down in a flap of
somewhere envelopes in somewhere drawers, to be
found
by relatives, who will wander these pages, somewhere
people
without labels or dates, stories only Alice could tell,
once real,
now somewhere in the past, soon to be deleted,
irretrievable.

Care

Care, they said,
You need care.
No care, she said.
But who will...?

I will, she said.
And how will...?
My way, she said.
But pain, they said.

The pain is mine
not yours, she said,
mine to know,
mine to challenge.

They go away,
frustrated,
concern rebuffed,
offers refused.

She sighs.
Wheels teacups
one at a time
to the kitchen,

stands painfully
turns on the tap
with two hands,
washes the cups.

Clanging bells

She says she is in a place she has not been before,
where the head is like one massive toothache,
where pain takes up so much room that hearing
is all gone, sight will soon follow. No music,
no books, she needs subtitles to read my lips.
Pills merely take the edge off, morphine sits in a jar
by the bed, her ticket to a night's sleep.

Communication her greatest need, each time I call
there is a letter to post, emails to show, each one
costing more than the last in eye strain, stiff fingers,
straight thinking, and misunderstanding.
Those thoughts. They spin in that swollen brain.
With nowhere to go they feed on themselves,
grow big and out of shape. They fill her days.

Minor spats like clanging bells that ring
in her head for days. One by one she turns them off,
daughter, sister, niece. Misconstrued, isolated.
She wonders what she said, why they snap back.
She reads her words again, finds them faultless.
Could she be wrong? Tears fill her eyes, her misty,
lonely, half seeing, inward looking eyes.

Alice's feast

It was all too much.
Red faced and swollen,
having so far a fielded a son
who arrived late again,
showered her with gifts,
grandson who vacced the lounge,
even on Christmas Day,
Alice fills me in
with kitchen instructions.
I make tea to slow her down,
but she talks and talks.

The oven is replete with bird,
roasts, soup, sauces. Dishes
lie in wait, steaming under foil.
She lists their contents
as if I were a novice,
apologising for not managing
what she has managed so well,
flitting between rooms,
and she talks and talks.

We adjourn to gift mode.
She insists we open them
so she can watch, excitement
bouncing her wheelchair, and
amplifying our faint praises.
She tries to find TV channels
to engage us, as if we might be
bored or short of amusement,
and still she talks and talks.

In a confusion of pleasure and pain,
unable to relinquish control,
she directs me to cutlery,

place mats and oven controls,
till we arrive at the super abundance
on the table, too small for such
a feast, too much for so few,
and the reminiscences begin,
as still she talks and talks.

Unable to enquire of us for fear
of not hearing the answers,
she fills our munching silence
with tales of the past, present,
but no future, praising children,
friends, parents, surprised at
our inability to eat more,
apologises for not doing enough,
as we struggle to keep up
with both food and words,
as she talks and talks.

In the post feast fug of fullness,
Dave tries to read his gift book,
I escape into the chores, hearing
her offering more to eat,
rolling on through her litany
of disabilities, in the over loud voice
of the deaf, in case we might think
less of her for things not done,
without legs, hands, ears and eyes,
but brain and tongue though in pain,
the last organs still unimpaired.

Something missing at the church.

Words from the vicar to comfort the faithful
but only one of faith here and she was silent.

Words from a life he never knew, from a family
he had just met, from a time before his.

Words of hymns no-one knew, mouthed
with lips and no voices, to an unloved god.

Words of a verse he thought she liked
from the son buttoned up with grief.

Words at the graveside lost in the wind
mired in winter mud and watery sun.

Words of solace between cold tight lipped
friends staring at the wordless silent box,

filling an earthy hole, as Alice once filled her
earthy life to overflowing with words.

Alice the healer

There never was a day when her greeting
was less than cheerful, always laughter, free
of rancour for my lateness, cup of tea
ready to boil, biscuits, buns, perfect
cakes, baked by imperfect hands.

There never was a day when the tale
was less than lively, less than full, even
though full of pain, full of struggle,
never tears, when the medics failed
again to impress or relieve.

And whenever I arrived, tired and low,
my own petty troubles, full of woe,
she would find me out and turn me round,
lift me up and gently put me down,
she in need of healing, healing me.

To the memory of RJ, with love.

Lightning Source UK Ltd.
Milton Keynes UK
02 December 2010

163737UK00004B/9/P